ASTRONUTS

ASTRONUTS:

SPACE JOKES AND RIDDLES

Compiled by Charles Keller
Illustrated by Art Cumings

11566
Simon and Schuster Books for Young Readers
Published by Simon & Schuster Inc., New York

Simon and Schuster Books for Young Readers
Simon & Schuster Building
Rockefeller Center
1230 Avenue of the Americas
New York, New York 10020

Published by the Simon & Schuster Juvenile Division
SIMON AND SCHUSTER BOOKS FOR YOUNG READERS
is a trademark of Simon & Schuster Inc.

Manufactured in the United States of America

10   9   8   7   6   5   4

Library of Congress Cataloging-in-Publication Data

Keller, Charles.
    Astronuts: space jokes and riddles/compiled by Charles Keller;
illustrated by Art Cumings.
        p. cm.
    Reprint. Originally published: Englewood Cliffs, N.J.: Prentice
—Hall, c1985.
    SUMMARY: A collection of jokes and riddles about outer space,
including "Where is a cinnamon man from? Outer spice."
    1. Outer space—Juvenile humor.   2. Wit and humor, Juvenile.
3. Riddles, Juvenile.   [1. Outer space—Wit and humor.   2. Jokes.
3. Riddles.]   I. Cumings, Art, ill.   II. Title.
[PN6231.S645K44 1988]
818'.5402—dc19 88-1919 CIP AC
ISBN 0-671-66290-2

For Barbara, Carol, and Connie

What does an astronaut do when he gets angry?
He blasts off.

What's moon juice called?
Craterade.

What's E.T.'s favorite year?
19E.T.5.

Why do astronauts blast off at noon?
Because 12 o'clock is the time for launch.

**Remember, spaceship, when you land on that
planet and meet their leader, don't laugh because
he's only 12 inches tall.**
How do you know that?
We've been informed he's a ruler.

Did you hear about the new invention that lets astronauts look through the walls of a spaceship?
No—what's it called?
A window.

Could you get me a ticket for the next trip to the moon?
Sorry. The moon is full now.

I heard you want to become an astronaut. Do you wanna fly?
I sure do.
Wait. I'll catch one for you.

What do you call a Russian three-year-old who explores outer space?
A cosmotot.

What happens when the sun comes out at night?
Oh, that'll be the day.

What did E.T.'s mother say to him when he got home?
"Where on earth have you been?"

Hello, spaceship to ground control.
Come in, spaceship.
I have good news and bad news. The good news is that there is life on Mars. The bad news is that we owe them rent.

Our engine just went out. I'll bet half the people down there think we're going to crash.
Half of us up here do, too.

How does Han Solo get from one spaceship to another?
Ewoks.

Who is Darth Vader's wife?
Ella Vader.

What do you call a moon that isn't hungry?
Full.

Where is a cinnamon man from?
Outer spice.

What's the last word in rockets?
"Fire."

What do you call a race track in space?
A star track.

If the sun is on one side of the earth and the moon is on the other, where are the stars?
On T.V.

What happens when Darth Vader misses three pitches in a row?
The empire strikes out.

Look out the window and see if the blinkers on the spaceship are working.
Yes-no-yes-no-yes-no.

On my last trip to outer space, I lived for a whole week on a box of crackers.
Wow, how did you keep from falling off?

We discovered oil on Venus.
Wonderful. Now we can buy a new spaceship.
We'd better get the old one fixed. That's where the oil is coming from.

What does a Martian take when he is dirty?
A meteor shower.

What do you get when you cross a spaceship with a magician?
A flying sorcerer.

What do you call a spaceship that is always sorry?
An Apollo G.

What did the astronaut say to congratulate his computer?
"Data boy."

What do you get when you touch a Martian frog?
Star Warts.

We're right on course. Below us now is Egypt and that's the Nile River.
Great! We hit the Nile right on the head.

Since I returned from the space flight, I keep seeing spots before my eyes.
Have you seen a doctor?
No, only spots.

Did your father help you with this problem in astronomy?
No, I got it wrong by myself.

Dad, how do those spaceships stay up in space?
I don't know.
What kind of fuel do they use in the rockets?
I don't know.
Am I bothering you with these questions?
Of course not. If you don't ask questions, how will you learn anything?

How are the Russians helpful to us in the space race?
Without them, we wouldn't know if we were ahead or behind.

Why do you always whistle on the spaceship?
To keep the Martians away.
There aren't any Martians within a million miles of here.
Sure works, doesn't it?

Captain, we're going faster than the speed of sound.
What did you say?

Why don't they put bucket seats on spaceships?
Because everyone doesn't have the same size bucket.

Why don't they have elephants as astronauts?
Because they don't have space helmets big enough to fit them.

What space creatures wear the biggest space helmets?
The ones with the biggest heads.

Who made the first spaceship that didn't fly?
The Wrong Brothers.

Imagine you were on a strange planet surrounded by strange creatures. What would you do?
Quit imagining.

Look, the people down there look like ants.
They are ants. Our spaceship didn't take off yet.

Why is being an astronaut a strange job?
You have to be fired before you can work.

Science has made fantastic strides in the last decade.
Yes, it's now only fifty years behind the comic books.

What is a comet?
I'm not sure.
Don't you know what they call a star with a tail?
Oh, sure. Mickey Mouse.

Why will we never see a full moon again?
The astronauts brought some of it back with them.

If your spaceship were traveling west, what would you see on your left hand?
My fingers.

How do astronauts sleep in their spaceship?
With their eyes closed.

I'm always sick the day before a space flight.
Then why don't you leave a day earlier?

Where did all the rocks on the moon come from?
Probably from an ancient comet.
Where is the comet now?
It went back for more rocks.

What did the space scientist find in his frying pan?
An unidentified frying object.

How do you like riding in a spaceship?
Oh, I have no room to complain.

**Try to drive our spaceship carefully. It scares me
when we land.**
Just do what I do. Shut your eyes.

Where do astronauts keep their handkerchiefs?
In air pockets.

Can you prove the earth is round?
I don't have to prove it—I never said it was.

I hear that on that planet they drive unusual invisible cars.
What's so unusual about an invisible car?
You don't see one every day.

What did the boy say when the extraterrestrial left?
"E.T. come, E.T. go."

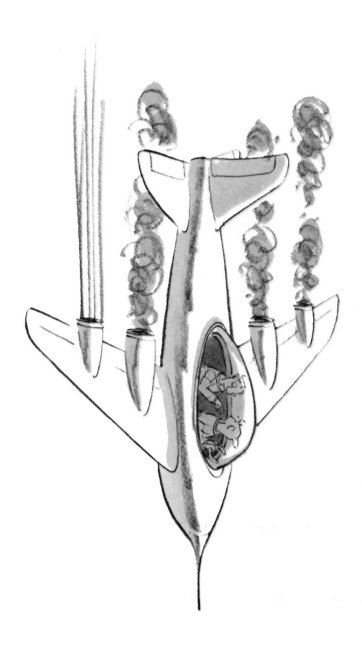

What made you become a sky diver?
A four-engine plane with three dead engines.

Why does the moon go to the bank?
To change quarters.

What can you see at a planetarium?
An all-star production.

Which is heavier, a full moon or a half moon?
A half moon because the full moon is the lighter one.

Why do you say that new astronaut isn't too smart?
He just went to the Naval Observatory to have his belly button examined.

If an athlete gets athlete's foot and an astronaut has missile toe, what does a moon surveyor get?
Two square feet.

Why did Mickey Mouse take a trip to outer space?
To find Pluto.

I'd like to study the stars.
Good idea. I'll get a map of Hollywood for you.

What do astronauts argue about?
Who gets to sit by the window.

How do you find the atomic weight of moon rocks?
Atom up.

What is the baseball version of Star Wars?
"The Umpire Strikes Back."

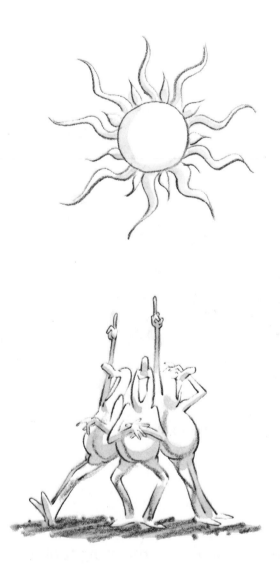

Did you hear the joke about the sun?
No.
Never mind, it's way over your head.

What did the baby planet say when it broke out of orbit?
"Look, ma, no gravities."

Before Pluto was discovered, how many planets were there?
The same number there are now.

What's the noisiest thing in space?
Shooting stars.

There will be an eclipse of the moon tonight. Are you going to watch it?
Sure—what channel?

What dish is out of this world?
A flying saucer.

**I heard about a man who went into space on
Sunday and came back three days later on Sunday.**
Impossible. How could he do that?
His spaceship's name was Sunday.

Which is closer, the moon or England?
The moon.
Why do you say that?
Because I can see the moon.

Who was the first man in space?
The man in the moon.

Why did the cow jump over the moon?
Cold fingers.

Which tastes better, a steak or a shooting star?
A shooting star because it's meteor.

What's another name for an astronomer?
A night watchman.

What kind of food do astronauts eat?
Launch meat.

Mom, can I go out and watch the eclipse of the sun?
Okay, but don't stand too close.

I failed every subject except astronomy.
How did you keep from failing astronomy?
I didn't take astronomy.

The sun is made of helium.
Why do you say that?
It rises every morning, doesn't it?

How would you describe the rain on that planet you visited?
Little drops of water falling from the sky.

When I travel on the space shuttle, I can look out the window and watch the sun rise.
That's nothing. I can sit at home and watch the kitchen sink.

What goes "Mooz?"
A spaceship flying backwards.

What's purple and orbits the sun?
The Planet of the Grapes.

Does the sun affect weight?
Sure, it makes daylight.

What would you get if the man in the moon fought Taurus the Bull?
Steer Wars.

Who served Yoda at his favorite restaurant?
Darth Waiter.

What kind of knots are tied in outer space?
Astronauts.

How can you tell when you've gone through the Milky Way?
It's passed-your-eyes.

This spacesuit fits you like a glove.
That's the trouble, it should fit me like a spacesuit.

What do you call the man who fires all the rockets at the space center?
Sir Launchalot.

Doctor, since I returned from outer space my ear rings all the time. What should I do?
Get an unlisted ear.

Hello, ground control, I have good news and bad news.
What's the good news?
We're traveling faster than any spaceship ever traveled before.
What's the bad news?
I don't know where we are.

Did you know that they found bones on the moon?
Wow, I guess the cow didn't make it after all.

What's the fastest way to get to the moon?
Climb into an elephant's trunk and tickle him.

Tell me how fast light travels?
The same way slow light travels.

What do the creatures on that planet eat?
Anything they can find.
But what if they can't find anything?
Then they eat something else.

What kind of bugs bother spacemen?
Astro-gnats.

What travels around the world without using a drop of fuel?
The moon.

How many successful landings must an astronaut make before he graduates?
All of them.

What did the astronaut say when he was asked about flying saucers?
"No comet."

Are you sure there are no hostile space creatures on this planet?
Yes, I'm sure. The Martians scared them all away.

As an astronaut, what qualities do you look for in a friend?
He should be down to earth.

What do you say to a 1,000-pound space invader?
I give up.
That's right.

What's the difference between the moon and the sun?
They're as different as night and day.

We're ten miles from earth.
What direction?
Straight down.

A space creature came up to me and asked me for a quarter to eat.
Did you give it to him?
Yes, and he ate it.

What did the moon-boy say to the moon-girl?
"Isn't it romantic? There's a full earth tonight."

How did you find the weather on your first trip to Mars?
I just looked around and there it was.

What do you call it when the earth goes backwards?
Revearth.

Did you know that there's a star called the Dog Star?
Are you Sirius?

In what school do you have to drop out in order to graduate?
Parachute school.

If the sun were famous, where would it go?
To the Hall of Flame.

What is the most popular phone company in space?
E. T. and T.

Are you tan from the sun?
No, I'm Tommy Jones from the earth.

Why are spaceships made of metal?
So you can tell them from jellybeans.

I just got a job working on the switches at the space center.
Is it a steady job?
No, it's sort of on and off.

Walking on that planet is very strange. Every time I took a step forward, I went two steps backwards.
At that rate, you would never get to where you're going.
I know, so I turned around and walked the other way.

Why is an astronaut like a football player?
They both want to make safe touchdowns.

What's green, likes peanuts, and weighs two tons?
A green elephant from Mars.

I'd hate to be 10,000 miles up in space in a spaceship.
I'd hate to be up there without one.

Were the questions on the astronomy test hard?
The questions were easy. It was the answers I had trouble with.

How do you get to the Planet of the Apes?
By banana boat.

I just read a down-to-earth story.
What was it about?
The last space flight.

Light travels from the sun to the earth at 186,000 miles a second.
So what! It's downhill all the way.

On the last space flight I didn't sleep for ten days.
Weren't you tired?
No, I sleep nights.

Last night I dreamed I got to spend a week at the beach.
So what? I dreamed I won two tickets on the next space shuttle.
I hope you invited me to go with you.
I tried, but your mother said you were at the beach.

What's red and squishy and wears a black mask?
Darth Tomato.

ABOUT THE AUTHOR

Charles Keller is a popular author of humorous books for young people. This is his thirtieth book for Prentice-Hall; earlier collections include *Grime Doesn't Pay: Law and Order Jokes, Norma Lee I Don't Knock on Doors: Knock, Knock Jokes,* and most recently, *What's Up, Doc? Doctor and Dentist Jokes.* Humor and folklore, both contemporary and traditional, have always fascinated Mr. Keller, a native New Yorker who now lives in Union City, New Jersey.

ABOUT THE ARTIST

Art Cumings' clever drawings have enlivened many books for children, including *Please Try to Remember the First of Octember* by Dr. Seuss. Mr. Cumings also illustrated a previous book of humor by Charles Keller, *Ohm on the Range: Robot and Computer Jokes.* He lives with his family in Douglaston, New York.